GW00808545

ON LOOKING DOWN

ON LOOKING DOWN

ON LOOKING DOWN

Audrey Brassington Stacey

The Book Guild Ltd
Sussex, England

The Book Guild Ltd.
25 High Street,
Lewes, Sussex

First published 1997
© Audrey Brassington Stacey 1997
Set in Times
Typesetting by Southern Reproductions (Sussex)
Crowborough, Sussex
Printed in Great Britain by
Bookcraft (Bath) Ltd, Avon

A catalogue for this book is
available from the British Library

ISBN 1 85776 176 6

I found this poem in a Bible when attending a Spiritualist Church in Sheffield, Yorkshire, where I was born, and was told to keep it as it would help me in times to come.

The Silence

Come, enter into the Silence
Close the door on the outside world.
And here in the blessed stillness,
Find the peace of the Spirit unfurled,
Till it wraps you around like a garment,
Healing and staying the strife,
Bringing a fresh new courage
To conquer the battles of life,
Life giving power of the Spirit,
Limitless, boundless and free,
This you will find in the Silence,
If you hold faith's golden key.

M. Hatherway

I have never held a certificate for all the healings that have been done through me, as one cannot put a material certificate on a pure spiritual force, which comes from other dimensions. The healings were always given freely, as it is a god-given force or gift to be used as such, knowing at all times that, if misused, this gift could be taken away.

ACKNOWLEDGEMENTS

My grateful thanks to many dear friends: to Mrs Betty
E. Pouton for the title, to Mrs Gill Cook for the typing
and encouragement, to Mrs Betsy Taylor to remind me
of my happy childhood, and to Mr R.R. Hedges for all
his support.

1

Where does one begin to write about the wonderful happenings in one's life, knowing that truth is stranger than fiction? As a child I had colour in my third eye (known as 'the cyclop', in the middle of the forehead) which used to comfort me as I fell asleep.

I had a happy childhood in Sheffield with my parents Elsie and Oscar Hibberson, who gave us, my older sister Eileen and me, loving discipline, as we could be naughty at times. We had one Saturday penny a week to spend and another if we drank senna pod water, soaked overnight at the week-end (ugh, this was not very often, thank goodness).

Mother was clever and made lovely dresses, coats and undies, knitted skirts and tops in wool which fitted perfectly and shorts with pleats to wear when we went rambling in the countryside. She dressed us both alike and people thought we were twins! Eileen was brainy and studied a lot. I was artistic and did knitting and crochet etc., for which Mother taught me to use my right hand. I used my left hand for writing and embroidery and both hands to play the Hawaiian guitar.

Daddy always told us to be good girls when we were young, as he said that he would always 'get our wavelength' if we had been naughty. We used to giggle but knew our faces would give us away. Mother's older sister, Auntie Gertie, used to say that I had healing hands when I was only 13, as I would put my hands on her legs and pray and she said that it always gave her ease.

There were often musical evenings at home. Mother played the piano, Daddy acted out humorous monologues. There was Ernest Vessey, a lovely violinist, Mr Chadwick, a pianist, his wife who was a soprano, and Miss Williamson, a lovely contralto, with a voice like deep velvet. Often Eileen and myself would slip out of bed and creep downstairs in our nighties, to sit on the bottom stair and listen to all the beautiful music. We were spotted, allowed up a bit longer, then sent off to bed.

The local operatic society used to put on productions. Once Daddy took a part at ten days' notice playing 'Rinaldo' in an operetta to stop the show from folding, as a singer had been taken ill. The Croft House Operatic Society presented him with a silver-knobbed walking stick with the inscription:

C.H.O.S. to RINALDO
14–19/2/22

Eileen and I used to carry trays of chocs and ice-cream around the audience in the intervals. Such happy days!

I remember one very bad incident at school when I was young: a teacher caned me across my left wrist for writing with it. The result was a big red weal, so painful it made me sob. I could not rest my wrist when writing. I returned home, and when my mother saw it she was distressed for me and furious with the teacher. She took me to the education office the next day, asked to see the director and said that she wanted me transferred to a decent school where left-handed children were not caned, as it had made me very nervous. Mother was the first to pave the way for other mums! So away I went to another school, where I was happier.

Another episode sticks in my mind: Eileen went on a country walk with a young man called Brett (I think) and when she came home later she said she would like me to dress like her and take her place the following night. After much pressure and not wanting to be a spoil-sport I agreed (a country walk in those days was considered very safe). I kept talking about the flowers etc. and dodging him, as he had wandering hands. He said, 'I cannot understand it, you are quite different to last night.' So then I told him I was not my sister! He still wanted to date me, but I said, 'No thanks.'

* * *

For the last ten years of his life, Daddy struggled to keep going, suffering with asthma, which I also inherited, so I knew what he was going through. He was asked if I would like to work in the printing department of the company where he worked. All was well until the telephone rang one day, when I had left Daddy at home, ill with what he jokingly said to me was 'tummyache'. I lifted the extension in the office and heard, 'Tell Audrey to go home, her father has just died.' I spun round and left the receiver dangling. My mother was devastated, as my sister was also in bed with colitis and enteritis at the time.

The day Daddy was cremated, snow abounded but the sun shone. Mother told me afterwards that Daddy had got out of bed to go to the toilet and she saw a bright light come into the kitchen from a dark cloud. She heard a cough and a bang and flew upstairs, knowing

3

he had gone. He was 49 years of age. The only consolation was that he was out of his suffering.

Eventually we pulled through. Eileen took a post in London and Mother ventured into a little business as a herbalist, selling drinks, sweets, ice-cream etc. I decided that she was so game that I would go and help her. The hours were long: from 7 a.m. to midnight. Often I would have to 'sweep' people out of the shop, but we were happy.

One evening, just before the war in 1939, I had my 17 remaining teeth out by gas. The lady surgeon was very upset as she had to give me an extra whiff of gas because I was coming round. The next thing I remember was being laid on my back on a long table and someone saying, 'Thank goodness she is coming round.' I saw the trolley tops of a tram car through the window and thought I had gone to heaven! I had lost a lot of blood and was in bed for a week. Soon after this, one lunchtime, Hibby (as my mother was often called) was having salmon salad and I poured on some vinegar. I had eggs, sherry and milk; my staple diet as I could not chew! Suddenly Hibby said, 'Audrey, that is the tastiest meal I've had in years,' and started to laugh. I had used whiskey instead of vinegar! I was without teeth for nine months, as in those days the gums had to harden. I felt like a toothless old witch! When the war came I had gleaming white dentures and was very glad to be able to chew and bite again, even though food was rationed.

2

During the Second World War my mother and I took a shop on Bath Parade in Sheffield, five minutes' walk from our house. We were put under 'Northern Command' (very hush, hush) and we gave our sugar ration to the confectioners across the road so that the troops could have a scone with their cup of tea. Tea was 2d a cup, and you were supposed to get 240 cups to a 1lb packet of tea! We pooled ours to give a good 'cuppa'! Boys back from the front (Libya) would come in and ask for 'Hibby' and Audrey, and said that ours was the best 'cuppa' in Yorkshire. Fame at last!

One day, one of the young men was taken ill in the shop, so we brought him through and laid him on the couch. I held his hand whilst Mum phoned the CO. He arrived and said that John would have to go to hospital. John said to me, 'Please do not let them operate on me, I could not stand another op.'

My reply to this was, 'OK, do not worry, I will help you.'

His parents lived down south, and travel was impossible for civilians, so I was given the go-ahead to stand in for them. John was taken to the huts which were put aside for soldiers who were injured. A surgeon came, and when he saw John he said that he would operate! My reply was, 'Over my dead body, as I have

5

the authority to stand in for his parents.' The surgeon disagreed, so I said, 'I will have your guts for garters if you dare touch him with a knife, and I'll take you to court too.' Pregnant silence. He stormed out. I went to John and sat down, put my hand on his forehead, held his hand and said, 'Go to sleep, relax, all will be well.'

Every afternoon, my dear Hibby would let me take the tram journey to the hospital to give John healing. I thanked the Lord for letting me in (I had no pass!) and for being able to give John healing. He once said, 'I never stay awake to say thank you,' and the man in the next bed said, 'You must love him a lot.'

My reply was, 'I am doing what is asked of me.' I could not tell him the Lord had pushed me, as a humble instrument, to do his work in healing John. The nurse used to bring a cup of tea for me and said it was a miracle. No-one had ever stood up to the Czech surgeon, Hertzog, who was known as 'the Butcher'. He was kept out of my way. John recovered, went back to his unit and was posted. I never saw him again. Hibby was worried I would be ill, dashing to and fro, but my reply was, 'Not to worry, the Lord will look after me.' He did, and still does.

* * *

A Mr Thorpe (CID) came to see us during one bad raid on Sheffield to check that we were safe. I had sprained my ankle that day, and we were busy, so he gave me healing and told my dear Hibby that I had the wonderful gift of spiritual healing and would be protected at all times. This developed as time went on.

'Doodle bugs' whizzed overhead in another bad air

6

attack. Hibby and I stood underneath the staircase because previously a soldier had asked if he could come through and shelter by the fireplace: he suddenly said, 'I advise you two ladies to leave and head for the hills.' And off he shot! We stayed underneath the stairs, as we thought it would be safer! Suddenly I was impelled to move and saw to my horror an incendiary bomb firing just above us. I shouted to Hibby, 'Hurry out, we've been hit. I will get a soldier to bring a sandbag.' I saw a very young soldier outside and asked for help. All hell was set loose outside, like Dante's *Inferno* — fire everywhere. The young soldier said, 'Duck, love. Where's your tin hat?' Between gasping for breath and ducking to avoid being hit, my reply was, 'I am a civilian and not issued with one!' Luckily we got back and he dashed up the stairs and put the fire out. In the rush he had lost his cap so Hibby gave him some money, as a Private does not earn much and we were so glad the fire was out. The hole in the attic had to wait until later. If humans, like cats, have nine lives, then I had used up one of mine!

We both felt that we had been protected, as we were both still alive. On looking at the incendiary the next day we found an 'Armstrong' marking on it — our English make! Nothing was said about the raids on Sheffield, as Hitler thought he had hit Attercliffe, Tinsley and Rotherham Steel Works, when in reality his German fliers got the 'Golden Mile of shops' where we lived. We never knew how many were killed, and I suffered from shellshock every time the guns fired, resulting in bad asthma attacks, which was to be my cross in life.

I did concert-party work at night after the shop closed, sometimes going to the miners, who were so appreciative. When I ended the evening playing 'Silent

Night, Holy Night' on my Hawaiian guitar, they sang in harmony, and it was so beautiful I had tears in my eyes. The miners wanted an encore, so after a promise that they would help me to catch the bus back to Sheffield, I played and the singing was even greater. So much feeling; surely the heavens heard, for we were protected from the bombs.

Another time that stays with me is when a lot of Italian prisoners were housed at Lodge Moor Prison Camp and the concert party was sent to entertain them. On this occasion, I finished with 'Aloha oe' and as a final encore my 'Silent Night, Holy Night'. Imagine the wonder when the prisoners stood up and shouted *'Bravo, bravissimo'* to me. The thought came to me that music could help to bring peace, even to so-called enemies, who as a whole did not want war. I did a lot of concert-party work for charity and entertained the troops before they went overseas. So many never came back. We always said that the cream of the country was lost in the beginning, as we were so unprepared. We must hope this never ever happens again!

3

After the war, Hibby decided to sell the business and go into retirement for a rest as we had both had enough. We went to the other end of the city where we settled in a semidetached house.

One day after recovering from an asthma attack I had a wonderful vision. Clifford, a dear friend of ours, a very gentle soul and wonderful pianist, had passed to spirit. He came through the closed back door into the living kitchen, paused, stood in front of me, smiled as if happy to see me, stood in front of Mother, smiled at her and walked through the closed door into the lounge as if he was going to play the piano for us. I told Mother and she replied, 'How lovely, dear.'

I discovered a wonderful way of knowing that the death of a person is so amazing when I had an out-of-body experience one night and saw my body in bed. The room was bathed in gold and I wandered around looking at the pictures on the walls. I looked at my body and was very happy to realise that there was no death! That we were to be given a life everlasting, as Jesus came back to tell the unbelievers; a truth so wonderful and yet so simple. Suddenly I heard a voice (my father, who had passed to spirit aged 49 years) saying, 'Audrey, go to your mother quickly, she is very ill.' I shot back into my body, gasping for breath, prayed for help and went to her bedroom and found her haemorrhaging from the nose, blood everywhere. I put cold compresses on her forehead and the back of her neck and raised her on pillows and cushions. I tried to get a doctor, but could not, as we had moved out of range of our previous doctor. I decided to keep on with the cold compresses, stripped the bedclothes, and put them into cold water. Eventually, prayer and help from the Lord helped me through all this, and Mother recovered.

We left this house because asthma attacks were getting me down and the doctor said the pollution in the air was the cause, so Hibby decided to try business life again — a drapery shop. On the day of the move I was so ill I had to cling on and hope and pray for help. The removal men were so kind, they got the bed up into our new living room, and Hibby put me to bed. Doctor Hope came next day — by this time I was stone cold from the hips downwards. The doctor said, 'She can't take much more, I will dash back and get an inhaler to relieve her.'

As I began to recover, I used to sit up in bed, doing the bills and orders to help my dear mother. Eventually she retired and went down south to my sister. I felt bereft, but knew that the promise I had made my father not to leave her was not broken. However, I knew she was not well.

Some years later, the police woke me in the early hours of the morning in my bedsit. Eileen (my sister) had rung them to say that my mother was very ill in the East Sussex Hospital in Hastings. I did not even know where that was (it could have been Timbuctoo!), so I dashed over to my boyfriend Bob's and asked him to take me to my boss's house to drop off a letter and the shop keys — I was manageress of a high-class sweet shop, with staff under my care. On the train I prayed and asked the Lord what was wrong with my mother. The reply was, 'Your mother has cancer of the stomach.'

Pale with shock I said, 'Oh no,' out loud.

Bob asked, 'What's wrong?'

I replied, 'Mother has cancer of the stomach.'

He then said, 'You and your Spirits.' His derogatory way of saying this reduced me to silence. After a long tedious journey we arrived at Hastings in Sussex and found the way to the East Sussex Hospital. I asked to see the sister in charge of my mother's case, explaining that I was the youngest daughter, from Sheffield, and had travelled down after a police message in the early hours of the morning.

When the sister arrived, I said, 'Sister, I want a straight answer to a straight question — has my mother got cancer of the stomach?'

She replied, 'Good God — are you a spiritualist? Your mother has cancer of the duodenum and pancreas!'

My prayer had been given an answer to help me over the shock. I stayed for one month helping the nurses. Hibby was a wonderful patient; the nurses and the sister adored her.

A letter came from Mr Bailey (my boss) to ask after Mother and whether I could go back to my job, as the under-manageress was due to go on holiday for a week. Back I came, as I was getting short of money — I did not get paid for that month, but when I said that I would quite understand if the under-manageress took my post, Mr Bailey replied that my job would be there when I returned eventually. So that was something to be thankful for.

After my under-manageress had returned, my uncle rang me at work to say that Hibby was worse, so off I went again, after seeing the boss who was kind enough to say, 'Do not worry, stay until you can come back. I know it is difficult for you.' Such kindness — I will always be grateful for Mr Bailey's understanding and that there are wonderful people who always help in times of stress. This time, I found a big change in my Hibby. Once I looked at her and found she had got a pair of scissors, and was trying to cut the tubes that were keeping her alive. I said, 'No darling, not that way,' and gave the scissors to my sister to take them out of Mother's temptation. She was getting so very tired. The last three weeks were fraught with anxiety and I was now praying for the good Lord to take her to the 'Garden of Rest'.

Every morning I would climb the hill and a gentleman who used to be in the garden said, 'Good morning. Have you someone ill in hospital?'

My reply was, 'Yes, my dearest mother is dying of cancer. Could you please sell me a few pansies, she loves them so much.' He gave me a beautiful bunch and would not take any money, and would wait for me every morning. Such kindness kept me going.

One day, a patient in the next bed, who was a Sister of the Poor, said, 'Your mother is dying, dear.'

'Yes, I know,' I replied. 'Is there anything you would like when I go out again?'

She said, 'I would love some oranges but have no money.'

So I said, 'Not to worry, I will cope.' Her face lit up so beautifully that I caught my breath and thought it was worth the sacrifice of the pennies. After all, money was only a commodity, like a chair or a table. The Sister of the Poor said, 'Bless you, my dear. I will pray for your dear mother and you to be given strength to carry you through.'

In Hastings I had bed and breakfast with two sisters

— they looked after me, and my sister when she was there, and they were so kind. I had lunch with Hibby in the hospital and stayed with her helping with the kidney bowl when she was sick, and cleaning her teeth, hands and face to give her comfort. She would then go to sleep after her injection. Once when she woke she looked so peaceful and happy and I said, 'Have you seen the angels?'

Her reply was, 'Yes, dear, and a lot more friends beside.' I dared not ask her if she had seen my father as I felt I was treading on holy ground. After Sister had been to see her one evening, Hibby looked at me with a twinkle in her eyes and said, 'I will have the last laugh on Sister when they carry me out of here feet first.'

I replied, 'Naughty, naughty. Sister thinks the world of you.'

We had a little laugh but I knew it was her way of telling me she would go, and once she said to me, 'I wish they would open those golden gates.' By this time I was praying for the good Lord to take her to the 'Summerland' as I called it. The last night, the sister would not let me stay, as she said it would be too upsetting and distressing. Back at the house I said to the two sisters, 'Oh! Mother has gone. Such a pain in my heart, like a knife sticking there.'

Five minutes later my sister answered the telephone and told me, 'Mother has gone.'

It was not until months later when walking through the woods that I broke down and cried! This was delayed shock, but I had to get on with life, and not be selfish and keep her spirit earth-bound. This happens to so many people who cannot let go of their loved ones. If only they knew that they do meet again in another sphere and took heart from this.

13

4

I went back to work in Sheffield, and later married Bob and went to live with his parents, who were as dear to me as if they were my own. When they became frail and bedridden in their 80s, I nursed them both, to the detriment of my health. I never dreamed of asking for help, but on doctor's orders I was sent to bed and given tablets. I woke up feeling dreadful, and went to the bathroom for a drink of water. Back in the bedroom I collapsed on the floor. Imagine my joy of joys when I saw my mother in spirit. She was dressed in white and looked younger and happy. We were laughing and so happy to see each other. Suddenly, she said, 'Audrey, you must go back, dear, you have work to do and so have I, but we will meet again.'

My thoughts were such that I did not want to go back — then my husband was trying to bring me round. I was in a death-sweat and very ill. He got me to bed and sent for the doctor who was upset and wanted the tablets back, but Bob had flushed them down the lavatory. The doctor was annoyed as they were very expensive, but when I told him of my experience and that I would not like anyone else to go through the same (as they would not understand, as I had, that there is no death — just a going forward to meet loved ones in another sphere) he went very quiet and patted my hand.

The second of my nine lives was gone.

Eventually, I went shopping one morning and prayed for strength. An elderly man raised his hat and said, 'God bless you for what you do, I see gold all around your head.'

I looked, smiled, and said, 'Bless you and thank you.' This gave me the strength to carry on. Mama Stacey (Bob's mother) passed on at Easter, a lovely soul gone, and Papa Stacey was heartbroken. The following months were spent in trying to keep him alive, as I knew he would not live long.

I used to take him out in a wheelchair into the woods to give him a break from the four walls. It was hard going as the chairs in those days were heavy! I would pray and ask for someone to help me, and always my prayer was answered as there was a steep hill to get to the house. Three weeks before Papa Stacey passed on, he said, 'This is the end of the road for me, lassie, and I do not know what you are going to do with our Bob. The d . . . fool does not realise you surround him with love.'

I replied, 'Please do not leave me. I will be lost without my dear friend.' However, as he passed to spirit I knew that my marriage would be on the rocks and that I would have to be very careful, as I remembered a conversation when Bob had made his mother cry and I told him to apologise. His father had said, 'If it had not been for your mother, I would have murdered you years ago.'

I said, 'What is all this about?' There was a long silence, and no-one spoke.

After Papa Stacey's funeral, we were told that the house was to be sold, so a dear friend, Connie (now in spirit), found a house to let in Ranmoor, in Sheffield, which needed a lot of cleaning. So I put my heart into papering and painting, hoping Bob would settle down.

Bob would go out at night, and I would go to church to get guidance and help and healing prayers, and also to develop my healing in the laying on of hands. I had a wonderful experience in one church. Mr Quastell, a Jew who was dedicated to healing, took my hand and lifted me off my feet, and a very deep voice came from him saying, 'You heal; many people benefit.' I was amazed as my feet had actually left the ground. I was gently put down and from then on I did more in the church.

One night we were sitting in a circle, praying for the sick. I opened my eyes and saw a blue ribbon on the knees of everyone. It stopped at one lady, broke off, and continued past her to the others. When we were asked if anyone had anything to say, I told them what I had seen and some of the others verified this. It turned out that she was the secretary in charge of church finances and had no spiritual connections like the others had. Others were saying peace was very much to the present company.

In Ranmoor, I met a lady who had a beautiful daughter, Pauline, who had polio. She was a very brave girl. She had a wheelchair and used to lift herself into her specially adapted car and go to work. Pauline and her mother came to see me when my marriage was in the balance, and we had lunch at my home. Pauline said that she would like to see my squirrel, 'Bobtail' as I called him (he had only a wee stump for a tail, as if his mum had pulled him back in the drey). So between us we packed a low stool with cushions and, with her back against a kitchen cabinet, put a woollen blanket over her knees and thin legs to keep her warm. I gave her some monkey nuts in their shells and said I would try and get Bobtail to come. I opened the kitchen door and shouted, 'Bobtail, Bobtail, come along, someone to see you.' He came to the doorway and looked at me, and I said, 'Bobtail, go very gently up Pauline's legs as she has poorly legs. She has some nuts for you.' He walked up very carefully, so quietly, sat in her lap and shelled and ate the nuts she gave him, then he let her stroke him. He then walked gently down the rug, took one look at us and left. I am sure the dear little Bobtail knew she was not long for this life. Pauline said, 'Thank you, Audrey, so much.' I never saw her again. Bobtail was right — she was not long for this life.

One morning my friend, Enid, asked if I would go and see her. Her husband had a seminar at the university and she said she would not be able to go as her eyes were bad, which usually resulted in her being in bed for a fortnight in a darkened room! When I saw the state of her face, all swollen and inflamed, her eyes so puffed up that she could not see, I asked how this had happened. Enid then told me that she had caught a germ in her eyes a year ago in Spain and the doctors and specialists were unable to find the cause or a cure.

I said, 'Sit down on this stool and let me give you some healing.' By this time I had put a white cotton mask on my face, covering my nose, as I was allergic to Enid's cat and dog and liable to have an asthma attack.

Enid replied, 'I do not believe in this.'

Suddenly I was hearing a deep voice saying, 'Sit down and close your eyes.' I prayed with all my might and found my hands were then trying to break down the heat of her face by waving in front of her eyes until I could get my hands over her eyes. Then I asked the Lord to heal her. My hands went to her head and whilst this was taking place her husband came into the room.

Enid started laughing, and said, 'I am not laughing at you, Audrey dear, I'm laughing at my husband's face. See you later.'

I was still semi-conscious and knew that someone very strong and tall was in control, so Enid had a healing for the whole of her body. Afterwards I gave her a blessing and said, 'All will be well.' Her husband came through for his coffee, so I said, 'I have been giving your wife some healing. Would you link up with me at 10.30 p.m. each night for it to be a permanent healing?'

He said, 'I don't know about that.'

In reply came a deep voice: 'If you love your wife you will. That is all that is required.'

He then said, 'Fair enough, I will,' and took his coffee into his study.

I turned to Enid and said, 'I do hope your husband will not take umbrage, as I have never met him before and it was the healer who spoke to him.'

She replied, 'Do not worry, it will be all right.' Whilst we were drinking our coffee I saw her eyes go back to normal. They were sparkling, and her face had lost the red inflamed and swollen cheeks. When her husband came back for a second cup of coffee he took one look at Enid and said in amazement, 'Good God, your eyes and face are normal.' He turned to me and said, 'Thank you. I will help.' I tried to apologise for what my healer had said and he replied, 'Not to worry, it is understandable.'

After that he would always escort me home, taking his dog for a walk, as it was often after midnight. He said, 'For what you have done for my wife, someone should protect you on these dark nights. I would not like anything to happen to you.'

I saw Enid months later in her car, and she stopped

19

and said, 'I have had no more trouble with my eyes since, thank you, dear.' I then asked if she believed, and she said, 'No.' I brought that sorrow down to Devon with me, but it was resolved years later, as I will describe in Chapter 8. To Enid and Bernard Clayton; I send you my love and blessings if you still live in Ranmoor. Should you perchance read this, I hope all is well with you.

5

I had many sleepless nights over my husband, Bob, going out and coming in late, but one night stands out in my memory. He brought a girl in and introduced her as Joy! I took one look and thought, Oh no. I sensed that what I had felt about my marriage was soon to erupt. He asked if he could have half the house for his girlfriend (who was 16 years old) and I the other half. I told him there would be no red light outside the house! Furthermore, my landlady had the temerity to tell me that the police knew about this girl and this had put me on my guard. Joy then said that if she could not have him, she would commit suicide. I thought this was emotional blackmail but as my husband, Bob, had a violent temper, I had to be very careful.

One night Bob and I had an argument. He now had a room somewhere where they went and he had taken a table and four chairs out of the kitchen, unbeknown to me, which had been a gift to me from him! He tried to make out that Joy was a good girl! I replied, 'What! With the hanging breasts and fat body of a woman of thirty who has lived, don't give me that twaddle!' This must have been a spirit using me, as I had no intention of saying this. A fortnight later he came in and said, 'You know, what you said about Joy was true.' He looked so pale that I thought, Poor devil, he has had a shock, so I told him to be careful!

One evening there was a wicked storm which lasted hours. I was on my own again, and I always watch storms, but this time I got a bit tired of the constant thunder and put the radiogram on to hear Semprini at 7.30 p.m. — he was a favourite of mine. Suddenly forked lightning struck at my feet as I was sat in my chair. I was petrified, as suddenly it hit the socket in the wall and blew up the radiogram! Dead silence reigned and I realised how lucky I had been. All Bob could say was, 'Is the television OK?' He told me I was hysterical. The repair man came the following evening, verified my lucky escape and told Bob I was lucky to be alive. I had used the third of my nine lives.

One night, after so many sleepless nights worrying about Bob, I asked the Lord at 5.00 a.m. to please help and give me sleep. Suddenly there was an indentation on the bed by my right side, an arm around my shoulders and a voice saying, 'Sleep my child, do not worry.' I had an hour of healing sleep — it was so wonderful. Was it my dear father?

Later I was watching the television and my husband came in early and said he was bringing Joy to the house. I replied, 'Over my dead body.' He came towards me in a violent temper, and I picked up my cross in my hand and mentally said, Please Lord protect me from him. I was so scared inside I did not know what to do. He kicked the door and the skirting board and raved but I kept very quiet. Eventually, he opened the door, banged it and went out of the house. I stumbled to the front door, saw the car had gone and decided then to pack his clothes in a suitcase and all his tools in a box and put them outside the front door with a note telling him to go to his friend Joy, whom he had chosen. I bolted the front and back doors, went back into the lounge and prayed to be protected. Suddenly, looking at the lounge window I saw a cascade of gold falling like a waterfall. I dared not blink and held the wonderful vision for as long as I could, then suddenly it was gone. The strength I received from this vision helped me through the next day. Later, Bob told me that he was tempted to strangle me, he was in such a rage. Perhaps this was the fourth of my nine lives!

Bob came back to see me and said that he had brought a letter for me to give to our landlady, Miss Hinde, and would I read it. It was to say that he would like me to have the tenancy of the house, as he was leaving. I asked several times was he sure this was what he wanted, as I did not want any more scenes. He replied that it was, so I took the letter the next day to Miss Hinde and she agreed to let me stay. That same night Bob came back and said, 'Have you given the letter to Miss Hinde?'

I said, 'I did as you told me.' He was furious! Eventually he left in a tearing temper again. After that, I would not let him in, as I could not stand the pressure and worry.

One morning I saw our family doctor in his car and flagged him down. He went around the corner and opened the door for me to sit inside. I told him what I was going through and how frightened I was of Bob and what he was doing. The doctor looked at me, took both my hands, held them, patted them and said, 'Did his parents never tell you about him?' I said they hadn't. The doctor sighed and said, 'Well, it's water under the bridge now. I am going to speak to you as a father would to a daughter. Get away from there, get a wee job and see if you can find a modicum of peace and happiness away from it all, you deserve better.' I thanked him, and asked if Bob was a schizophrenic. He did not reply but wished me all the best. What a good friend he was.

So I got a job in a newsagent's shop from 8.30 a.m. to 5.30 p.m. then walked to the wine shop below and worked there from 6.00 p.m. to 10.00 p.m. having taken sandwiches and a flask of tea to keep me going. The newsagent's shop was hard work but I was happy. I found my solace in going to the Spiritualist Church to pray for guidance and was always given a warm glow of feeling before a message came through. One night a visiting medium said that she would like to speak to me after the last hymn, for what she had to say was for my ears alone. She came to me, held my hands and said, 'My dear, what you are going through was not of your making and the suffering you are going through should never have been your lot. "They" are telling me to say to you that you must *never* take him back, as they can heal your breaking heart once but could not do it a second time.' My weight had dropped from ten stones to seven stones with the shock of it all, and this made me realise that the doctor's advice was right.

It was indeed, for Bob did try again to come back. I told him that he could get on with his own life and I would get on with mine! I also told him to give up smoking, as he would end up with cancer if he was not careful!

24

6

After some time I went to the centre of Sheffield for a job, which gave me more experience. I ended up in the fashion department of Pauldon's which had shops within a huge complex. My job was selling raincoats and expensive furs; the latter were locked up behind heavy plate-glass doors. One day a lady from another shop came and asked me if she could try on a mid-length ponyskin coat. It was beautiful, but when I helped her into it, I went stone cold. She asked me what was wrong, as she saw me turn pale. I told her that I could 'see' the pony running across a field and felt dreadful. She then said, 'It is not your fault and you are not to blame, it will go to a good home.' I must admit the coat did suit her, but I could not wear one knowing how I felt. Within half an hour I sold another one and still felt the same. My boss was very pleased, but I felt I would rather sell raincoats.

Some weeks later I saw the same woman (Mrs S.) again and she showed me a lump with a red ring around it on the right side of her neck over the jugular vein. I put my fingers on it and prayed for healing to take place. She knew what I was doing and we would meet in the corridor, or link up in prayer at night in the sleep state. She had been to the doctor's previous to this, and told me he had made an appointment for her to have an operation. When next we met at work she said, 'Look, the red ring has gone, the lump is smaller, but if I go into hospital next week I feel I shall not come out, as I have had so many operations and do not want another one.'

My reply was, 'Do not worry about this, we will pray about it and let the good Lord take over.'

All that night and the next day whilst serving customers I asked for protection for her and no operation. It was bitter cold weather and snow was falling. I had quite a job to get to work, and was wondering about Mrs S. when she came into the department in her coffee break and said, 'Our prayers were answered.' She then told me that she was lying on a cold bed in a white gown, shivering, as the heating was off, due to the intense cold and heavy snow. The surgeon greeted her with, 'Mrs S. I believe, you are to have a leg off!'

She then said, 'I shot up in bed and said, "Oh, no it is the lump on the right side of my neck that needs attention." The surgeon took one look and said, "Don't worry about that. Look sharp and get dressed, go home and have a good warm!"' It turned out that there were two ladies of the same name in the ward at the same time. We had a laugh of relief and gave a big thank you to the Lord for the help and for hearing our prayers. The lump went after a few more healings. To have been used as a humble instrument in healings, with prayers being answered, was a miracle in my mind and always left me with a feeling of joy and peace.

On the way home I was slipping and trying to keep on my feet, and the snow was freezing fast. I found my way to the front door, took a spade and started to dig the snow away from the door so that I could open it to go inside. No sooner was I inside the front door than I smelt gas so badly that I had to put my scarf over my nose. I went straight through to the back door and opened it wide, went to the landlady and asked her if she would telephone the gas company, as the gas had filled the house, even to the attic. At 10.00 p.m. they arrived and started digging outside, then came into the house and said, 'Madam, there is enough gas in this house to kill 14 men!'

I replied, 'Yes, it feels like it, and I suffer with asthma.'

He replied, 'Open all the windows in the house. I see you have had the sense not to plug anything in.'

I said, 'Thank you, but if this continues I will be a corpse.' We laughed but this was the fifth of my nine lives gone. A big mains pipe deep outside had cracked. The gas had seeped into the cellar, up into the kitchen, up the stairs into the bedrooms and then into the attic!

* * *

Whilst at Pauldon's I met a dear friend, Ruth, who suffered from emphysema and had healing to ease her. I knew she was very ill, so we helped where possible, letting her live as she would like to, having fun with barbeques in the country. Ruth asked if I would be her companion on a trip to South Africa to see her sister, as she felt the journey would help her. Sadly, I knew that this was not to be, but said that if at all possible I would be there. A fortnight later, her dear aunt came into the shop and told me she had passed to spirit. I was glad for her sake that she was out of her suffering, but sad that Ruth had not had her last wish gratified.

A letter came from a friend, Elsie, who lived in Brixham, Devon. In her letter I read, 'Audrey, I feel you

27

are in deep distress. "Dare to be a Daniel", apply for a job at the holiday camp for a summer season. You could always stay with me.' The idea of 'Dare to be a Daniel' was a challenge, so I wrote to the Dolphin Holiday Camp, sent photos, and was accepted. I was always fond of dolphins.

I gave in my notice at Pauldon's to Mr Davies, my boss, who was very upset and wanted to know why I was leaving. Briefly, I told him of my upset, and that I wanted to start a new life on my own, away from my husband. Mr Davies replied that he was sorry to lose me and that there would always be a job for me, should I return. He said he quite envied me going to Devon. We parted with a hand-shake and good wishes. I was very surprised when the staff had a collection and gave me going-away presents.

On arriving home, after I had sorted my thoughts out, I went to see my landlady and told her I had taken a job in Devon for the summer season. I said I would lock the house up, and on no account was she to let my husband in or tell him what I was doing, or where I had gone. I said I would pay the rent once a month to keep the house for me when I returned at the end of the summer. I did not get any money from my husband, so he had no hold over me. My landlady said that she was quite envious of my going and wished me luck. I think that by now she realised I was not to blame for past events!

7

I came to Devon on a 'Prayer and a Song', knowing that
I had a job to go to and somewhere to stay in the camp.
It was a traumatic time, being amongst strangers and
trying to keep a stiff upper lip, but I decided to think
positive and see it as an adventure. I knew that I was
being looked after, as my faith had led me with the help
of my friend, Elsie. My sister, Eileen, had written to say
that she felt I was in need of protection and told me to
buy a cross. I bought a gold Cross of Iona and a fine
gold chain later when I had saved enough money.

Whilst working in the Dolphin Holiday Camp, I met
some very nice visitors, who used to take me for a run in
their cars on my day off, which helped to take my mind
off the past. I also used to get packed lunches from two
sisters who worked in the catering department. They
told me that if I was going down to St Mary's Bay I was
to tell Dick and his wife, Elsie, to give me my tea, as this
was included in my wages. I loved to sit on the sands
and watch the tide come in, to gain strength from the
serenity and peace there. I remember the thick ham
sandwiches which tasted so good.

My friend, Elsie, whom I used to visit when off duty,
was taken very ill, due to trying to stop a dog attacking
her dog in her garden. She must have pulled the
muscles of her heart. The last night I saw her, I asked

29

her husband to send for the doctor, who made her climb the stairs! I said, 'Don't do that. Can't you see she is dying, and should not be moved?' I had to go back to camp, although Elsie wanted me to stay, so I said a fond farewell, knowing I would not see her again. The next morning Chris, her son, banged on my chalet door to say that his mother, my dear friend, had passed away later in the night. Another friend, Doreen, who was in charge of the linen for all the bedrooms, asked me what was wrong. When I told her about Elsie's passing, she said, 'Audrey, you can come and stay with me, I have a spare bedroom.' So I replied that if her husband agreed, I would like to accept her kind offer.

While I was staying with Doreen and her husband in Brixham, I thought that I would like to move to Devon to live. However, before taking the ultimate step I was told to contact a medium, who had a place in Brixham, so I made an appointment. The medium looked at me and said, 'I see you sitting on the grass surrounded by girls and boys and you are talking to them.'

My answer was, 'Yes.'

She then said, 'To get a piety within you, but you are not pious.'

Then I said, 'Excuse me, do you have a headache?'

She replied, 'Yes, a migraine.'

To help her I said, 'Hold my hands.'

'Oh, you have the gift of healing,' was her reply. To her, joy was instrumental in taking away the pain. The medium then said, 'You were talking to the young ones seriously.'

I replied, 'Yes, of my experiences as a healer and my belief that we are all given a chance to serve others in a good capacity and a good way of life.'

She then said, 'You live in Devon.' My reply was that I was working in the Dolphin Holiday Camp for the summer season. She then said to me that I would come to live in Devon, and that it would be an uphill struggle, but I would win through and a new way of life would emerge for me. Then she gave me the proof of what direction I needed to take. When I asked her how much I owed her, she would not make a charge, as she said, 'One good turn deserves another!' Another proof that I was being looked after from above.

I talked things over with another friend, Pat, in Brixham after her little boy had healing on his knees to strengthen them (he often used to fall when running). She suggested that her husband, Fred, would be able to hire a van for me to bring my furniture down to go into store. So with the help of another man from the camp and a few waitresses who were dropped off en route and who also gave me what they could afford towards the petrol, we all started on a hilarious journey back to Sheffield. Sunday was spent in sorting and loading the furniture I had before I was married: my books, records, personal wardrobe and contents, carpets and cooker. I left the rest for my husband and wrote him a letter to say I was leaving Sheffield and he could call on the landlady, Miss Hinde, for the house key and take the rest of the furniture. He had until the end of the month, as I had already paid the rent till then. My landlady was sorry I was leaving but said she could understand and wished she was coming too! Heaven forbid, I thought, with a chuckle! So started a new phase in my life, but oh the horror of trying to get off Spaghetti Junction in Birmingham nearly drove us crazy! In sheer desperation I said, 'Let's get to the next turning and keep going until we find a signpost on a straight road.' Both men heaved a sigh of relief when we were back on the road south.

I managed to get a job at Rossiters in Paignton, but

31

after paying for bus fares, bed and food, and for my furniture in store, I found I could not save. Doreen's husband also became a problem. I said to Doreen, 'I'm sorry, dear, I do hope our friendship will not be broken, but I will have to leave, as your husband is developing wandering hands.'

She said, 'Do not worry, Audrey, I know him of old!'

The strange thing was that later, when I got a flat in Dartmouth Road, he helped me move my few belongings in his car, and he said, 'I do hope you are not jumping from the frying pan into the fire because of me!' How strange that he should say that!

My reply was, 'That is something I must risk.' I knew the bus fares and the long walks up two hills at Brixham after being on my feet all day were taking their toll of my health and energy! So I thanked him, told him to behave and to give my thanks to Doreen; I would keep in touch with her.

One lunchtime I was sitting in the park in Palace Avenue eating my lunch, as the dust from the carpets caused my asthma to flare up. I saw a house opposite, fixed my eyes on it and mentally prayed, Dear Lord, I would love to have a first-floor flat, with a balcony, and do healing work for you.

A few weeks later I went to work at Marjorie Michael's fashion shop, where the work was more interesting and there was more fresh air to help my breathing. My landlady, Mrs Brown, had decided to go abroad for Christmas and her dog was taken to the kennels. I was glad of this as I was allergic to animals too. I was on my own in my cold flatlet, no central heating in the house, and I developed a nasty cough. To crown it all, there was a snow blizzard outside and the electric meter was taking 50-pence pieces as if there was

32

no tomorrow! I decided to go to bed to try and keep warm, and to relax to help my breathing, as my inhaler was not working as it should. Suddenly, whilst I was dozing, a coldness came into the bedroom and hands were clutching my throat. I struggled, grabbed my Celtic cross in my hand and held it up in front of me and said out loud, 'In the name of the Father, the Son and the Holy Ghost, get thee hence.' There was a 'whoosh' of very cold air and I realised it had been an evil entity or force at work, which resented me. I thanked the good Lord for protecting me as I realised my sixth life had gone.

I carried on working, and my faith kept me going. A week later, Gypsy Phil, a true Romany, came into the shop and Marjorie Michael said, 'You go and see her.' She was afraid of gypsies.

I asked Phil how she was and she replied, 'Better than you, dearie; you are in great trouble.' She then described what I had gone through that night the previous week. She then said, 'I will cast a spell to get you out of there, the sooner the better.' I bought some flowers from her to cheer me, and thanked her.

On my day off, another Brixham friend, Hazel, came to see me and said that the flat would be the death of me. My reply was that it nearly had been. When I told her what had happened and what Gypsy Phil had said confirming this, Hazel went on to say, 'I know you are ill, could you put your hat and coat on? I will help you and we'll walk slowly to meet a lady, Mrs Gregory, in Palace Avenue. We will see if she can help us.' It was a first-floor flat, furnished, but old and worn, so I asked if she would kindly part with the old furniture and keep the best, as I had some very nice things in store and would make the flat very nice. She agreed, but asked if I would keep a sideboard and a very big trolley which

33

stood on the landing.

Mrs Gregory wanted me to move in the next day, so I asked my boss, Marjorie, if she would let me have the day off if I worked extra time in the next two weeks to keep everything straight. Marjorie agreed, as she was worried about my state of health.

The morning I left the Dartmouth Road flat, I remembered Gypsy Phil's spell. I was to put salt in my hand and as I went out of the flat, throw some of the salt over my right shoulder and then, as I went out of the house, throw the remainder over my left shoulder. This I did, remembering her words about leaving the entity of evil behind!

I was so relieved and glad to leave the place and to know that my prayers had been answered. Furthermore, another prayer had been answered, as the flat I moved to at 46 Palace Avenue was the one with the balcony on the first floor that I had fixed my eyes on, whilst having lunch in the little park. Who says prayers are never answered? Mine were, more quickly than I dreamed possible. Miracles do happen through Jesus!

I had to attend Torbay Hospital for a check-up and got the 'all clear'. Wonderful happy years followed with Dot, my landlady, and Mrs Aylen, who had the top flat. We became good friends, and she wanted me to go on holiday with her to Austria, which I would have loved but had the feeling it was not to be. Mrs Aylen had a dainty gate-legged table, flaps down when not in use, and I used to tease her when she said, 'It is for my son!' Ann, as she then became to me, said that she had had her son before she married Mr Aylen. The boy's father had walked out on her, and Mr Aylen had brought him up as his own. So I replied that it made no difference to me, as she was a good person and still my very dear friend. Not long after, I saw her sitting on the stairs, and said, 'Ann, are you all right, dear?'

She replied, 'I feel so ill.'

I dashed down the stairs and held her and she died in my arms. Dot went for a neighbour and we got Ann on to the settee downstairs; she looked so happy and peaceful and young. What a wonderful way to go to meet her loved one in spirit. Why did she tell me about her son? To make her peace, I guess. The son and his wife came and were so shocked; both had bad headaches, so I gave them tea and healing and said if they needed help to call on me. They both came down and said that they had no room for the little gate-legged table and would I like it, as Ann had said what a good friend I had been! I had tears in my eyes, as I told him how we used to joke about it. Always when I polish it, I feel that Ann is around.

I began to go to meetings in a 'Little Upper Room', as I called it in my mind, over the Conservative Club at Preston. An hour before the service was the time for healings for those who needed it. Mrs White, (Flo) the medium, became a very good friend. One evening, after the healing session, a man came up and asked if I had a certificate for healing. Flo very quickly said, 'Mrs Stacey does not require a certificate for healing.'

I said, in a very quiet voice, 'Jesus did not have a certificate and you cannot put a material certificate on a spiritual force which comes from the Lord, knowing at all times that if it is misused in any way, it could be taken away and one has to be very careful of this!'

One Sunday evening the visiting medium did not arrive. Flo asked if I could take the meeting, but I felt I was unable to. A visitor came up and said in a deep voice, 'Excuse me, I am a visitor on holiday, also a medium, can I be of use?' We had a beautiful address, then I suddenly went warm and glowing. Flo announced the last message, but the medium turned and said, 'Just one more. I must give this to you.' He pointed to me and said, 'Can you take the name of Oscar?'

My reply was full of joy. 'Yes, it is my father's name, bless you.'

He then said, 'He is holding a silver-knobbed stick in his hands and dancing for joy to see you here and is happy for you.'

I replied, 'Thank you for the proof of this, as I have waited years for this wonderful happening from you as a stranger, and Joy and God bless you.' No, it was not telepathy as I was not even thinking of my dear father. I danced for joy that week, my feet and body felt so light.

8

On a visit to Yorkshire, I stayed with a friend, Bessie Burley, who had remained a friend through the time when my heartbreak was worst. She suggested I rang my other friend, Ann, whilst I was with her. I rang Ann, and when we had asked each other how we were, she said to me, 'Audrey, did you know your husband was dead?'

I replied, 'No, when did this happen?'

Ann then said, 'I will send you the cutting out of the paper if you will give me Bessie's address.'

This I did, and thanked her. By this time, I was in shock. I went to Bessie, who looked at me and said, 'You look dreadful.'

I said, 'Ann has just told me over the phone that Bob is dead!'

Bessie brought out the Malibu (a rum and coconut drink) and said, 'Drink this, it will do you good!'

Suddenly, I started to laugh, and said to Bessie, 'Bessie, I should be in the Guinness Book of Records — divorced and widowed in one minute on the telephone!' I had never been served with divorce papers, and did not divorce Bob as I could not afford it. After all, he was the guilty party. Bessie took me to the Town Hall and we found the death certificate of James Robert Stacey, aged 71 years, dearly loved husband of Joy.

When I showed my marriage certificate, it was quite amazing the consternation on the face of the registrar. It shook me when I later rang Norman, my brother-in-law, and he said that Bob had died of cancer.

My holiday with Bessie was meant to be, so that I could learn all this, and we still keep in touch by letter — another proof of being looked after by friends both earthly and heavenly. It shook me to remember that I had warned Bob if he did not give up his smoking he would die of cancer. I would not have wished this on him, in spite of his wayward life and the anguish I had been through at the time.

* * *

After Ann passed away, Dot let the flat to Evelyn, who became a friend. She had two men friends, and I am glad to say Reg won and she was married later. Reg had a sister who came on a coach trip with us to Compton Acres. All the time we were there I tried to catch up with her as I knew she was in great pain from her leg. On the coach I went and sat next to her and said, 'I have the gift of healing, would you let me put my hands on your knee?'

She just looked and pulled her skirt up and said, 'Here, take it, I've had enough.'

As the coach was moving, I quietly prayed and asked for only the highest and the best to work through their humble instrument to heal the knee. Suddenly I felt a movement on the knee-cap under my warm, still hands and knew that there had been an adjustment by a higher source. Then I said, 'When you walk across the crossing by the Central Church, don't worry if you feel hands on your spine, it will be the adjustment whilst you are walking.' She thanked me and said that she

38

would put her stick away when she got home.

On a visit to me later, she said, 'I've been painting and decorating the flat since I saw you on the coach, and also what you said about the church happened to me.'

I said, 'What was that?' and she reminded me of the 'hands on the spine', which has stayed with me ever since. I felt so humble yet so happy to be used in this way to help people. Her brother, Reg, and Evelyn were amazed, as I had said nothing about it, but they were delighted too.

Another day I arrived home and my friend, Doreen (from the holiday camp), came to see me. She said, 'Audrey, help me!' I took one look at her throat; she could hardly talk, as it was black and blue. Her husband had tried to kill her! He used to drink heavily. She was given healing and then we had the usual cup of tea to help her get over the shock. After that she left him and had to get police protection from him, so apparently there was no hope for him. Doreen has since married again and is happy. I am so glad for her, as she deserves a better life.

One morning, at work, I was putting garments back on display in the window when I saw a lady looking in. I smiled at her and she came in. She then said that my smile had drawn her in, so we gathered dresses, skirts, blouses, costumes etc. and as we were walking down to the dressing-room she said, 'I see your mother walking beside you.'

I replied, 'Oh, how lovely. I wish I could see her.'

She then said, 'You will one day.'

As I was helping her into a dress, she said in a quiet voice, 'I am a medium.'

My reply was, 'I know you are.'

She then went on to say, 'They are telling me that you

with the help did a very good job of healing a lady's eyes in the Midlands!' Imagine my joy! Then she said, 'And furthermore, they are telling me to tell you *not to worry* any more, it is quite all right.' So that was how, years later, from a complete stranger, I had the answer to the sorrow of Enid not believing. How wonderful! There is no time limit in spirit; so often the years in between do not matter to them, and if an answer does arrive, we are so happy to get confirmation of our thoughts and prayers. It makes me realise even more how very careful we should be in what we think, say and do all the time

* * * *

I used to do my shopping at a little fruit and veg shop in Torquay Road, owned by a young couple, Peter and Carol, and baby Mark and mother-in-law, Rosie, who was looking very pale. When I asked how she was, she said that she had an ulcer, so I asked if she would like some healing. She came to see me and found benefit in the healing and today we are all firm friends. In fact Peter is like a son to me and he has often done jobs for me and would not take payment. Sadly the shop did not pay, so Peter changed his job and went to work in a bank. Peter told friends about the healing I do, and through this I met Betsy, who lives at Kingsbridge. So another healing started, and I met her husband, John, who made me very welcome and showed me around Kingsbridge. John passed to spirit and Betsy was so devastated that I tried to help her all I could by telling her about when I 'died', and saw my mother in spirit, and how happy I was and did not want to come back! We keep in touch and over the years have become close friends.

Whilst I was living in Palace Avenue, I did healing at night through being recommended by different people, and kept Sunday night for the healings in the church over the Conservative Club. One evening, while healing in the Upper Room, a young lady came in. She had lovely dark hair and was so serene. I knew at once she was the medium for the evening. She was very shy, so I introduced myself and found she was Sheila McCarthy. When Flo came in I introduced her. We had a lovely evening and Sheila is now a very good friend, and like a daughter to me.

1972 was a year to remember. One evening I was asked if I would see a Mrs Betty Pouton, whose husband, Eddie, had had a nasty stroke down his right side. She said, 'I don't care how long it takes, so long as my Eddie can speak again.' When Eddie came up those steep stairs and sat on the stool and I put my hands on his shoulders, I felt his heart beat so heavily that I just thought, Dear Lord, we need all your help. So commenced a long slow journey back. There followed months of patience, faith and prayers from everyone, and one night Eddie spoke and I said, 'Betty, he's done it, he spoke to us.' He walked with a bit of a sway but was so much better. To me this was so wondrous and I thanked the healers without whom we would be bereft.

That same year, I could not understand why my breathing was so short when I sat in the lounge in the evenings. A voice said, 'Audrey, there is a gas leak at the connection, do something about it!' I knelt down and sniffed, and there it was! I got in touch with the Gas Board and asked them to come on my day off as I did not want to upset the landlady. The man came and sealed the connection and said that there would be no more trouble. This was my seventh life gone!

41

Around that time I was asked to heal a little boy's eyes — the tear ducts were dry. The mother came, and then the father for a few weeks, and then there was no news. I still prayed for the boy; he was a lovely child, but so quiet. The sequel to this was years later when I had left Paignton to live in Preston. I met his grandmother, who started to tell me her plight, which she said was due to the boy's mother leaving her husband with the two children, as she had gone off with another man. The grandmother had been left to look after them. When I asked about the boy, she said that his eyes were now fine. Another answer to a prayer.

9

Years passed, and I was made redundant. As I was only three months from my sixtieth birthday, I decided to retire. By this time I was very tired and wanted to give myself more time for the healing.

Suddenly, a new phase started. My dear landlady, Dot, was taken ill and later passed to spirit and then I was offered £7,000 to move out. I wrote to the Housing Department, but they could not give me any satisfaction, although I had been on the housing list for years. Eventually, the house was sold with two sitting tenants. The new landlord wanted me to move up to the top flat, which did not have a bathroom, only a shower, which I did not care for. The landlord tried to pressure me by taking floorboards up in all my rooms, rewiring up and downstairs, but I put up with this as it was necessary. But when the front and back doors were taken off and a blizzard of snow came howling through, I became very ill with my breathing and was coughing a lot. I went to the doctor, and when the receptionists saw me they decided to transfer me to a Dr Macloughlin for treatment. He was so kind and asked what it was all about, and when I told him that I only needed two points to be rehoused, he decided that something should be done about this.

I was praying that I could be rehoused to start afresh.

Within six days someone came to see me, and I had to make up my mind very quickly what to take and what to sell and give away. Actually the new flatlet was so small it would have fitted in my large kitchen. Friends helped with packing, and Peter, who was like a son, helped with the carpets, fittings and measuring, as by this time I was so exhausted. Eventually, I settled in and started to do some healing. Oldway Mansion, a local beauty spot, was just across the road and I used to go in to absorb the peace and beauty of the trees and flowers.

On one occasion, a man came and sat beside me and as he was limping, I asked what was wrong. He said that his knee was playing up and he dreaded going to the doctor, so I asked him if he would like me to give him some healing, as it was a gift from God and freely given. He said that he would be glad. Healing took place and when I had finished I said, 'God bless you and peace be with you.' Then I asked him to walk away, turn round slowly and walk back. This he did and was so pleased, he said 'Inshallah.' Then I knew that the 'powers that be' had healed a Jew. I felt very humble.

Another time, I thought I would go for a little walk to look at the sea. I had just turned into Manor Road when a young lady got out of a van and started limping across towards me. I could see that she was in great pain, so I asked if I could help. I took her to a seat where she told me that she had come down for the day with her boyfriend, as she had just had a plaster cast taken off her ankle and nothing more had been done. After the healing, which she said was so soothing, I told her to put her foot to the ground. She was able to walk away, very relieved. It passed through my mind that Jesus must have done a lot of this in his life, and I always wanted to be used in this manner even if my plans for the day were altered.

10

Many years have passed, and my healing work has continued. In 1993, Betty's dear husband, Eddie, had a blocked artery in his right leg and Torbay Hospital thought that the leg would have to be operated on. Both Betty and I felt that Eddie's heart would not stand the operation, so we asked and prayed for healing in the sleep state each night. Once a week Betty took me to her home for the laying on of hands, with those from the Highest Authority taking charge. Eddie's big toe and two next toes went black, and the heel broke out. Dear Eddie was heavily sedated, for the pain was so bad. Later on, two toes started to heal and the heel began to get better. Months passed, then the hospital had another look at his leg and foot and felt that perhaps only the toe would have to come off. I could see both Betty and Eddie were getting very tired. Betty used to dress his foot when the nurse could not come, and this was upsetting, even though she was gentle. The pain for Eddie must have taken its toll on her too, so when Betty brought me home, I would give her tea and biscuits then some healing to help keep her going. That such lovely people have to suffer made me wonder why, yet I knew this was to test if we could still keep our faith and carry on, not being sorry for ourselves or bitter in adverse circumstances.

I told Betty that I felt Eddie was getting very frail; pain and drugs were taking their toll. In 1995, on 16 February, Betty rang; Eddie had been taken into Torbay Hospital with a massive stroke. I made arrangements to go with Betty to see Eddie several days later, but Betty rang the day before to say that Eddie had passed to spirit, which I had prayed for as I knew he had suffered enough. The cremation was on 6 March, a sunny day. Paula Mayer, the deaconess, gave a wonderful spiritual address. I felt honoured to be there. Both Betty and Eddie had done a lot to help charities. I did whisper to a friend, as we sat at the back waiting for the hearse to arrive, that I felt that when Eddie was fully restored to his new life he would be with the little children he loved so much, although he had never had any of his own. I smiled at the deaconess when she mentioned that Eddie would be helping the little children, as we both knew he would be happy doing this. Eddie had had his first stroke in 1972 and it was now 1995, 23 years on, so he had done well to get this far. As a doctor once said to me when I was young, three score and ten, and after that we are living on borrowed time! To which I said, 'From the minute we are born we are living on borrowed time!'

He replied, 'You could be right.'

Once, when I went shopping in Paignton, I bought some dates and nuts and, walking out of the shop I heard a voice say, 'Audrey, you have been short-changed of four pounds.' I went back, but the elderly lady in the shop denied this. I went further on to shop for wild bird seeds and nuts, still upset, and passed the shop on my way back. A young lady came out and said, 'Please come back. I am so sorry, you were right and here is the four pounds.'

I said, 'Thank you, as I only have my pension and

46

know how far my money will go!' Was my father, or my Guardian Angel, keeping an eye on me? I was so glad it was made right.

Since I have lived here in Brookfield House, I have found Adrienne (the warden), and her husband, Norman, to be very caring people. They do a lot to make the gardens beautiful, with the help of Barbara, their friend. The gardens are so beautiful at the front, in fact people come just to admire them. As I am now 79 years young and healthwise have slowed down, I trust in the Lord to send me people who need healing in my wee home. I have made many friends over the years, who still write to me, and life has had its ups and downs.

On Sunday 7 May 1995, I saw history in the making. The fiftieth anniversary of VE Day was celebrated; hands of friendship were joined and nations reconciled. Fifty heads of state from all over the world joined the Queen and her family and the public in the largest gathering to make a symbolic commitment to peace, and to enjoy a concert featuring tri-service massed bands, the European Youth Orchestra, the National Youth Ballet, a host of children's groups and a thousand-voice choir. All the heads of state followed the Queen, who was taken by two children to the World Map Dome to sign an olive leaf for PEACE and all the heads of state did likewise. To me it was so moving; there were tears in my eyes as I realised that the children of today were witness to this and that tomorrow's children, we hope, will have a better way of life.

I think a good way of closing my book will be with this little prayer which I pray every night, after Healing Prayers, to people I know:

Thank you, Lord for my lovely day.
Thank you, Lord for friends sent my way.
Thank you, Lord for the roof overhead.
Thank you, Lord for my comfortable bed.
Thank you, Lord for the birds and the
bees.
Thank you, Lord for the flowers and the
trees.
Thank you, Lord for giving me Love and
Strength through knowing Thee.

Let us live, O Lord we pray
In sweet content from day to day.
In lowly toil or simple pleasure,
May we find wealth enough to treasure.
Put Hope and Courage in our Hearts
That we may bravely play our parts.
Grant love and friends and peace of mind
And gratitude for blessings kind,
And when the sun sinks in the West,
Grant blessed Peace and Healing Rest.

Anon